Inspiring Visual RE
Colour supplement

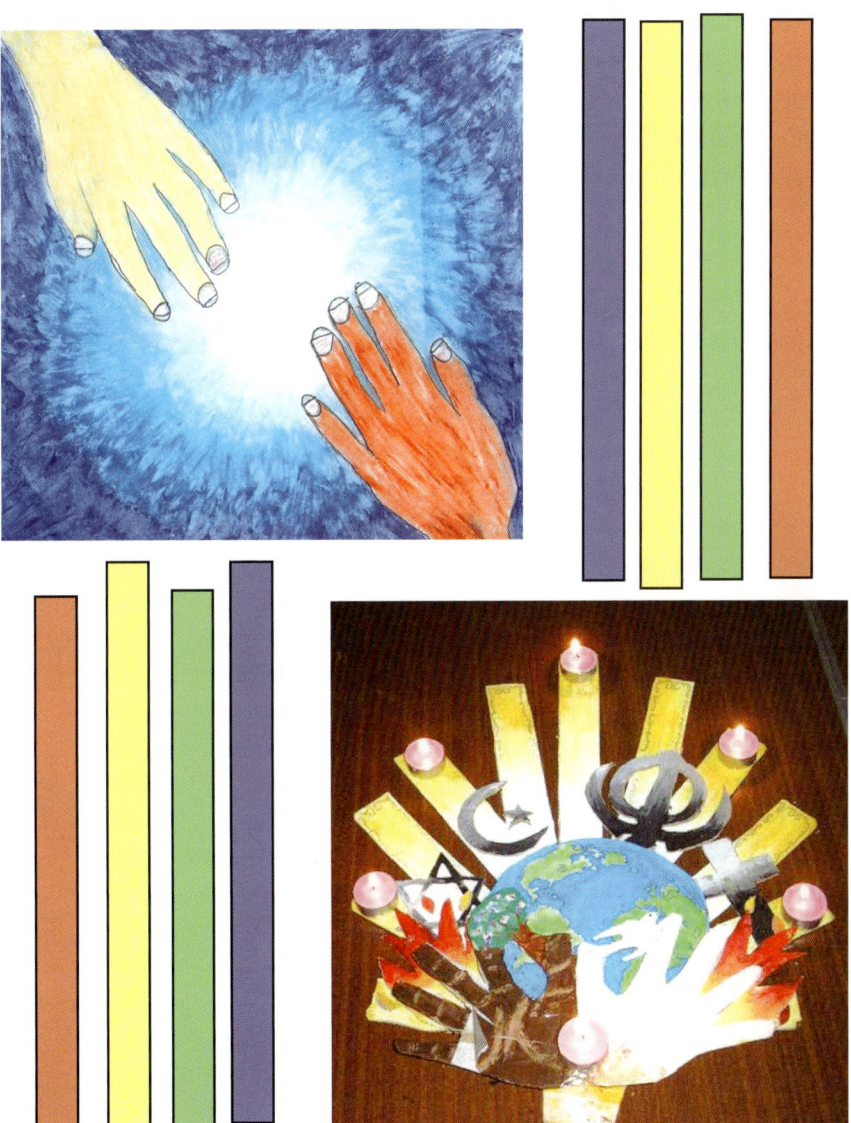

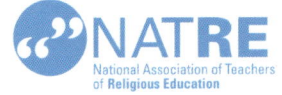

Spirited Arts theme:
Telling it My Way – Stories of Faith

God's Ladder, Jacob's Ladder
Molly, age 8

'I have drawn a pale figure to show that God is there but you can't really see him. The ladder is in the story of Jacob's dream. The ladder shows the levels from God coming down to people. It starts out bright and shiny, because God is like that, and it gets duller when he gets nearer to us.'

Heaven's Ladder
Sam, age 12

'Jacob had a dream of a ladder going up to Heaven (the story is in Genesis 28). It was a symbol of connecting with God. In my version, the steps are the things by which we hope to reach heaven – good works, sincerity, humility, faith, hope or love. But the rungs are no good without the sides, which represent Christ to me, so the only way to heaven is through Christ.'

Patterns: expressing the spiritual

'Stained Glass' as an inspiration: 1

Layla, age 8

This lovely 'stained glass' image has been created by Layla, an eight year old who offers images of different places of worship in Newham. They are all connected to the central image of planet Earth. The simple 'technology' of the plastic stained glass has enabled her to realise some deep spiritual ideas.

With real insight, Layla writes:

'God is light and all around the world. God is for everybody. God is in different places, and different forms for different people.'

'Stained Glass' as an inspiration: 2

Hannah, age 8

Hannah made her Art in Heaven image by cutting shapes into the pink sugar paper and making light windows of tissue paper stuck behind the shapes. Her moving picture is called 'Saying thank you for Mum'. She writes:

'I wanted to do a rose, and my mum, because my mum died a while ago and her favourite plant was a rose. I felt very creative when I made this. I am thankful for my mum.'

The Pearl of Nature
Pooja, age 11

'My image of a flower is to convey a message of peace and tranquillity. I used an engrossing technique to depict different cultures with different colours of rice.
I got the idea during an exhilarating RE lesson when I read a book called *The Red Tree*. In the book a girl wakes to find black leaves falling on her from the ceiling, and threatening to overwhelm her. She has to find a tiny red seed that will grow to save her. We discussed all the philosophical ideas in the RE lesson.
"The Pearl of Nature" uses a flower in red and green on a shining background to symbolize human happiness in a dreaming world. The blue glitter is for a dreamy effect.'

God is Always With You
Jennifer, age 15

'This is a question which is challenging and people find God in different ways and places and sometimes not at all. I based my design on my response/belief that God is everywhere. As a Christian, I believe that God is omnipresent and responds to individuals when they call upon him.
The person in the middle of the picture represents people who might feel alone and in need of help and guidance. The coloured strips of paper represent the Holy Spirit surrounding all people, even though they may not realize this. The words are verses from the Bible – God's word – that people might read to reassure them that God is always present to protect and guide them if they should ask for it: "Do not be anxious about anything. The peace of God, which transcends all understanding, will guard your hearts and minds in Christ Jesus."'

Patterns expressing the spiritual: learning from Hinduism

Traditional rangoli pattern made by Grace, age 10, using coloured sand

Rangoli patterns can be square, rectangular or circular, or a mixture of all three. Rangolis always have at least one line of symmetry. One side reflects almost exactly what is on the other side. This is a reminder of the Hindu belief in Karma. Rangolis are temporary; they are always swept away. This reminds Hindus of the transient nature of life.

Rangoli pattern: Cheltenham Bournside School

Artist Ranbir Kaur worked with Religious Studies, Maths and Art students to produce a 12-feet-square rangoli pattern on the floor of an art room.

The careful placing of the rice grains, seeds and pasta pieces required a slow and painstaking approach, slowing down the students and cultivating a total absorption with the process.

Students created a 'sacred space' around the installation using muslin drapes and producing suitable background music to encourage a meditative atmosphere.

© Martin Poynor

Patterns expressing the spiritual: learning from Tibetan Buddhism

Monks from the **Tashi Lhunpo Monastery** in India, creating a Tara mandala out of sand at the Museum of East Asian Art in Bath in 2008.

Within the Tibetan Buddhist tradition this is a highly developed form of meditation and art.

For an online mandala photo story go to http://www.meaa.org

© Museum of East Asian Art 2008. Used with permission.

Patterns expressing the spiritual: learning from Islam

The Muslim understanding of Allah

'This picture recalls the first revelation of the Holy Qur'an to the Prophet Muhammad (PBUH)

The 12-year-old artist has skilfully used collaged wool, foil, paper and colour to suggest the swirling, overwhelming presence of the Angel Jibreel, and the mind of the Prophet receiving the sacred revelation. Islamic rules prohibit the use of figures in this scene, but the artist has made a virtue of this necessity, as Islamic art often does, using pattern and colour to suggest the momentous events.'

Judges' comments

The Holy Name of Allah
Jade, age 8

Jade was inspired to make this by using a repeater pattern from the ICT equipment. Muslims are inspired by the holy name of Allah, Lord of the World. The painting uses Islamic rules, and does not picture the divine.

The Holy Name of Allah

Pupils working with Muslim artist Razwan Ul-Haq produced this beautiful piece of art. They first practised writing the word 'Allah' in different ways. The concept of 'God' in Islam was briefly discussed with the pupils: in particular the fact that Muslim artists do not tend to visualise what God looks like. This particular piece was a pupil idea of cutting up different ways of writing Allah in Arabic, and then putting it all together as a collage. The finished abstract piece faithfully represents the fact that, in the Qur'an, Muslims are reminded that there is nothing at all like God.

Spirited Arts theme: Where is God?

Up in the Sky
by Eliot, age 8

'My picture is about where I think God is. The balloons and kites are messages to God – like his mail, instead of a postman. This picture shows me where God is: not far away.'

Where is God? Everywhere
Georgia, age 10

'God is in all the beautiful things in the world. You can see God in animals, at the seaside, and in woods and birds. God is in your mind as well, to help you see him in everything else.'

God as Colour
Sophie, age 10

'In my painting I have shown God as colour. It means each different colour is a feeling or a mood. I like this idea because if you group all the moods together it makes God. I used bright colours because they mean happiness, joy and fun.'
Judges: 'This symbolic picture is one of the best metaphors for God in the whole of the competition, and Sophie is only 10. Beautifully thought out and beautifully made.'

Where is God?
Understanding Love
Lloyd, age 11

'My work is about God being everywhere and loving everyone. People think God is not around us.

I think they are wrong. If God wasn't part of everyone how would we understand what love is and what it means? I wanted to show this by showing God's hand reaching out to everyone's "heart".'

Where is God?
Your Request Has Been Denied
Penny, age 15

'"Your Request…" represents the feeling that God, if he exists, is unreachable and hidden.

At a time when we need God most, such as the peril the girl is facing, we reach out. No one grabs our hand. The masses of paper falling from the sky are a suggestion that our prayers never reach anyone. Cast up to the sky they fall back down again.

The phrase "Your request has been denied", written on every piece of paper, is a suggestion that I can't reach God. I feel there is no personal bond, no personal response to my prayers. All we receive is a weak cover-up of the truth, an automated message: your request to be happy, to be alone, to do well, to get better, has been denied. If this is what happens, I feel it is very unlikely that God exists. This is what my paint and ink expresses. The different coloured lines represent movement, the different feelings the girl experiences during each prayer, each denied request.'

The Lord is With You Always
Rowena, age 13

'God is in all my life. The picture's a mess: life is not tidy. CDs and my MP3 represent music. When I'm depressed, I listen to music, and this is a place that God is. School tie and books represent work. God is with me in everything. A scrap of paper from my notebook (which I use to help me make decisions) is in the bottom left-hand corner.

God is with me in the choices I make. Photos of my friends and family, my dad, the people I love. My cuddly toy, that I have with me when I sleep, shows that God looks after me when I'm vulnerable. My open diary shows that God knows everything about me. It also represents prayer: I sometimes use the diary to talk to God, to help straighten out things in my life.'

Open Your Eyes
Inayah, age 15

'The number of people in the world who call themselves atheist or agnostic is 850 million. These people either do not believe that God exists or are unsure. One of the main reasons that many of these people do not believe in God is because they claim to not be able to see any evidence of the almighty being. However, the girl in my picture represents these people who do not see any evidence of God, and her eyes are closed.

It is my belief that people who do not see the evidence of God's work in creation and design of the world need to open their eyes wider to see the sheer beauty of the world and the plain evidence that God does exist. From the beauty of the stars and the sky and nature to the amazing systems such as our own nervous, circulatory and digestive systems, God's remarkable skill is displayed everywhere.

My painting shows "God" written everywhere, and anyone viewing the picture can see this very obviously. It is just as obvious, by looking at nature, that God is everywhere, as is the evidence that he exists. The painting shows that there is evidence of God in absolutely everything and all we need to do to see it is to open our eyes wider.'

Expressing beliefs in artistic ways: a focus on the question of evil

God – He Lies In You

Jennie age 14

'People say that the presence of God is everywhere: I think that includes us. Every one of us possesses Him. My design includes a mirror: look at this artwork, symbolizing God, and see your own face. The image will be broken. It is hard to see that God is part of each one of us. Rays of yellow light bring a sense of happiness. The purple symbolizes spirituality and inner power. I have painted round the mirror with blue, a colour associated with heaven.

The design itself is like a stained glass window. It is a very personal thing and I am sure that not everyone agrees with my opinion. This design has deep meanings; everything from the colour to the shapes used symbolizes something. I will not explain what I intend everything to mean, because I think this is what discovering the painting is about.

The main message my picture carries is that we can only use our own inner power, and inner spirits, to guide ourselves to a happier life, to one day be accepted in whatever world awaits us after death.'

In the Balance

Luke, age 13

'We believe that God is the balance of life. He is like the scales of justice, of good and bad. You can't have life without both sides because you wouldn't appreciate good without the bad. Some examples are night and day, illness and health, famine and harvest, suffering and joy, death and birth.

If God answered all prayers and no bad things occurred equilibrium would be lost and we would never learn from our mistakes. He is the yin and yang of our existence.'

Spirited Arts theme: My Spiritual Life

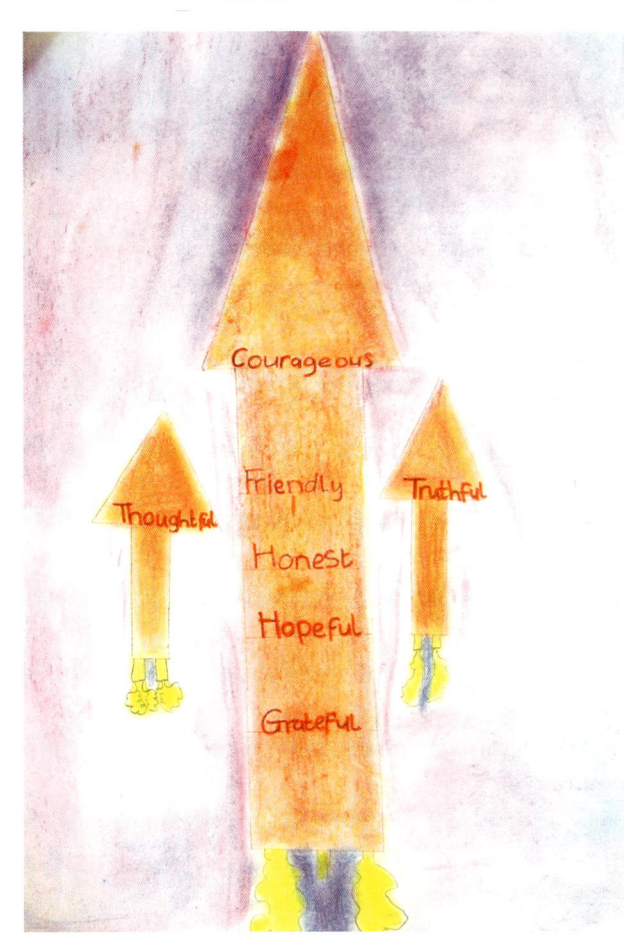

Three Rockets: My Spiritual Life
Conor, age 8

'My picture is based on the theme of "My Spiritual Life". I chose to do a picture of three rockets because they are a powerful image. In words on the rockets are how I feel inside, but I don't always do the thing on the rockets. The rockets are for truth honesty, hope courage, friendliness and gratefulness. I feel proud of myself. When I am older I want to be the sort of person that I think that I am now and to be like a rocket that everyone else can see.'

Spiritual Life
Siobhan, age 13

'Music, humanity, rainbows, God's good earth and people to love are the elements of my spiritual life. I have captured what people should value in the world, be grateful for what they have achieved and have spirit and belief in what makes them feel good about themselves. People being happy and celebrating life because they are not worse off for what they have: they have life; talents; gifts and each other, and this can make them happy and spiritual. For me spiritual life is being with my family and friends and sharing gifts and happiness and letting each other know that we are loved.'

My Spiritual Life
Isobel, age 12

'This is a representation of me and my thoughts and beliefs. In the middle is a photograph of me with different spiritual versions of myself coming out of my main body. Each is holding the symbol of a different world religion - Judaism, Islam, Christianity, Buddhism and Sikhism. There is no symbol for Hinduism because the main feature itself represents a Hindu belief: God appears in many different forms.

I show myself in different forms holding different religions because I do not belong to one religion; I simply believe and agree with different aspects of different religions. For example, I agree with the Buddhist belief that you are reborn as another living thing when you die and you could suffer due to wrong things you have done; however I am not a Buddhist. I feel that today so many people belong to different religions and I want to get the point across that it's OK to have mixed opinions.

To make my artwork I used computer graphics. I am proud of my work: it truly explains and represents me. In the background there are photos of different times in my life (my first day at school, me as a baby) all these things in my life have happened and my surroundings and the people I know have changed, but I stay true to my deep thoughts and beliefs. Different friends in the pictures belong to different religions and help me learn and understand about different faiths, allowing me grow as an open minded spiritual person.'

Spiritual Life: The Bird
Merina, age 13

'The bird in the centre of my drawing represents God's voice and spirit, projected.
The bird comes out of the human mouth: God's voice is projected through all that lives. The saxophone shows that the spirit of God can be represented in music. The painting of the girls says that God can be represented in art. Actions speak louder than words: God's voice can be heard in actions. The actual voice and spirit of God – the bird – contains six religion's symbols on it. Different religions worship in different ways, but I think they all have the voice of God. The writing on my bird symbolizes the prayers of all the people of all the religions: the word of God. Thank you for reading my evaluation of my spirited art. I hope you liked it.'

Spiritual Life: God Lights You From the Inside
Kim, age 11

'I believe that God is in your soul, in your heart, but most of all God is the light inside you. My favourite story is called "Footsteps in the Sand" because I truly believe that when you think God is not there, that is when he is carrying you. In my picture, I have drawn what I believe about God.'

Spiritual Life: The Soul in Space
Priya, age 13

'My picture shows a soul, which is the droplet of God that is inside every living thing. The soul is the real you. This soul is travelling, travelling through the space of the skies, to go to its next body.'

Spirited Arts

Along with some images to resource activities outlined in the accompanying curriculum books, *Inspiring Visual RE: Using and Making Art in Primary RE* and *Inspiring Visual RE: Using and Making Art in Secondary RE*, the examples of children's artwork included here will impress and inspire you. They show some ways in which RE in Britain enables children and young people to tussle with life's big questions, to show their own profound insights and to learn from different religions for themselves.

Spirited art in the RE classroom is never just 'draw a picture'. The competitions we have run over the last five years have always included themes from which pupils and teachers can select what stimulates them most. While we have used a 'story' theme every year, this has never asked for mere illustration. Our most popular themes have used a question about God: some RE practice still fights shy of 'doing theology' in the classroom, but these ideas have been enthusiastically received by thousands of learners. Many pupils have proved that 'visual learning + theology = profundity.'

This selection of imaginative and creative examples of RE are chosen to inspire you, and show you the depths of thinking and beauties of expression which young people in RE in Britain are producing.

The National Association of Teachers of RE has run an annual competition for more creative RE since 2004. 'Art in Heaven' is one of these initiatives.

Many thousands of children of all ages and abilities have entered their work in Art in Heaven, and the web gallery showcases some of the best. See genius at work at: www.natre.org.uk/spiritedarts

What would your entry for Art in Heaven be? How would your pupils benefit from these approaches?

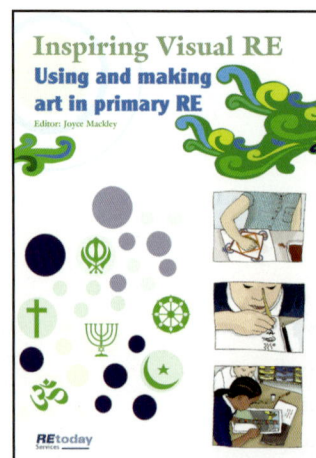 

All NATRE 'Art in Heaven' entries
© NATRE and artists 2008

Inspiring Visual RE
USING AND MAKING ART IN SECONDARY RE

For generations, faith and spiritual insight has been conveyed through the arts. Great works of art are visible ways of communicating the invisible. Creative talent expressed in art can inspire and move, and often connects us to something deeper – something spiritual.

When you look at the colour supplement with this booklet you will be captivated by the artwork produced by young people. Many are from the Spirited Arts competition run by the National Association of Teachers of RE (NATRE); others, from schools engaged in creative artwork linked to world religions. All have found exciting ways of using RE to unlock the insight and creativity of students.

This publication draws on this artwork to help you identify the power of using art to both stimulate and express deep ideas and beliefs. It includes some general approaches and is illustrated by two articles which illustrate the great learning that follows when schools actively combine the skills from the Art and RE classrooms – to the benefit of both subjects – but more importantly to the benefit of the student's own understanding and personal development.

Use the suggestions and ideas to help your students learn about spiritual expression in different faiths, and to express themselves spiritually. Be amazed at the insight, creativity and imagination they display while enjoying some great teaching and learning in RE!

Joyce Mackley
Editor

Weblinks

The RE Today website provides full colour versions of all the artwork included in this pack for use in your classroom, together with other materials. The password for access for subscribers can be found in each term's RE Today magazine.
www.retoday.org.uk

Look out for this symbol throughout the publication

'Spirited Arts' images and additional guidance can be found on the National Association of Teachers of RE website
www.natre.org.uk

Contents

	Page
Learning with images: nine ideas for the secondary RE classroom Lat Blaylock	2–6
Expressing beliefs in artistic ways: a focus on the question of evil Elizabeth Pope	6–11
Creating art: eight ideas for the secondary RE Lat Blaylock	12–15
Art as meditation: sacred and secular Stephen Pett	16–22
Recognising achievement and attainment in creative and artistic RE Lat Blaylock	23
Spirited Arts	24

Learning with images: nine ideas for the secondary RE classroom

For the teacher

How can we enable pupils to be good visual learners in RE? One approach is to use artwork by other pupils to explore and model ideas, issues, techniques and examples. Here are eight flexible ideas about how to do this. Any teacher spending half an hour with these ideas and images will come up with lots of ways to adapt the ideas to other themes, other art activities and other religious focuses.

This section refers closely to the images in the colour supplement. Page references in the form pC1, pC2, refer to pages in the supplement. The images are also available on a PowerPoint sequence at: www.retoday.org.uk

Three simple and general ideas

1 Writing and making art: match and make sense

Take the images and separate them from the pupil texts that go with them. Ask your pupils in pairs to do three things:

- Look at the pictures without seeing the texts, and devise titles for them; talk about which ones they think are best and why.
- Sort them into an order of preference
- Give out the texts that go with the pictures. Ask pupils to match them up. Do they want to change their order? What has the text added to their understanding of the images?

2 Prize winners?

Ask pupils to look at all the images, and make some judgements. Try the following reviewing and recording structure.

- Put prints around the classroom – on desks or on the walls.
- Place an envelope marked with the picture title and name next to each image.
- Give pupils 10 coloured cardboard squares to use for voting. They can give one token each to the 10 pictures they prefer, or several tokens to the few they think are the very best.
- Count up the tokens for each picture. Discuss the ways the images show pupils' skills and beliefs. Ask pupils: Did you choose pictures you agreed with? What is the difference between good art and good spiritual expression? Is all art spiritual in some way?

3 Organising images two by two: a way to reflect

- Place an even number of images on the table (10–16) and ask pupils to match them into pairs. Don't give them any criteria for this. Working out their own links encourages creative free thinking about the meanings and connections between the images.
- As each pair of pupils complete their pairings, they join with another couple and compare the ways they went about the task.
- Ask pairs to create a pair of paintings or images of their own. Try these antitheses to get them going:
- believer/doubter
- spiritual/material
- life/death
- heaven/hell
- light/dark
- good/evil
- love/hate.

Pupils' choice and creativity is stimulated by the initial sorting approach.

Six ideas for using specific pictures

1 Expressing the spiritual

Look at the images by Conor (pC13), Siobhan (pC13) and Isobel (pC14). These three young people show in their artwork ways in which spiritual life means something to them. Use these three to get pupils talking and thinking about the concept of the spiritual.

Step 1: Consider the three pictures What do they tell us about being spiritual? What does that mean? Are they similar or different?

Step 2: Look at lots of other images: postcards of artwork, natural world images, photos of people. Which do you find spiritual? What does the word mean to you?

Step 3: Discuss these three ideas of what 'spiritual' means. Which is best? Which worst? Why?

A 'Your spirit is what makes you a unique human being. It is like your fingerprint – you alone can say what your spirit is, and what it means.'

B 'Being spiritual is the part of being religious in your heart. If you are religious, then your spiritual life is your own thoughts and prayers, your own sense of God.'

C 'Being spiritual is about all of life – the Earth, other people, your own self and God. Everyone is spiritual in some ways.'

Step 4: Write your own definition of 'spiritual' in 25 words or less. Swap with a partner and see what you each think of the other.

Step 5: Develop another definition together, the best you can, using all this work to sum up.

Step 6: Claim your prize as the best describer of spirituality in the class. If you are spiritual, you will have to give the prize away to the most deserving person.

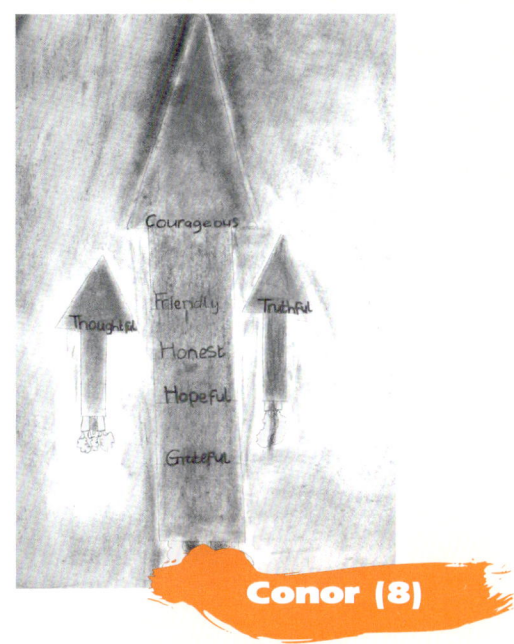
Conor (8)

Siobhan (13)

Isobel (12)

2 The spirituality of different religions

Students look at artwork from Merina (pC14), Kim (pC15) and Priya (pC15) and discuss with a partner what these young people believe.

- Can they find something about reincarnation, about God within, and God with us, about God in the different religions of the world and about God found in music, nature or prayer?
- What do the pupils think of these beliefs and how they are expressed? How do these beliefs link up to different religions?
- Compare the artworks by pupils with statements of Hindu belief, and argue the view that art expresses religious ideas more fully than words.

Merina (13)

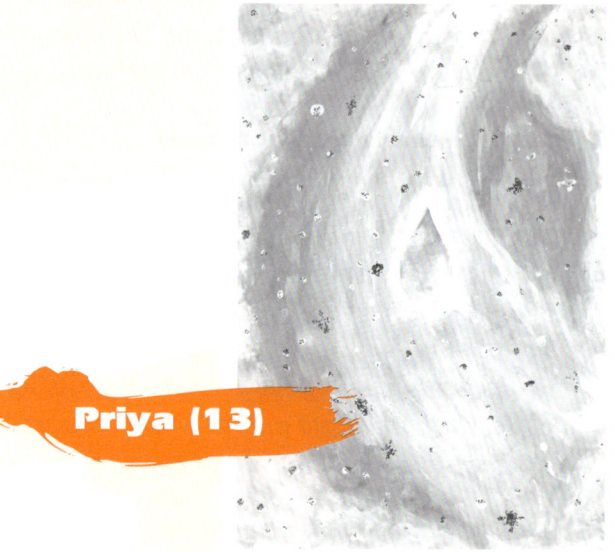
Priya (13)

Molly (8)

Sam (12)

Story in RE : Jacob's ladder

The story of Jacob's dream of a ladder connecting earth and heaven is full of meaning and allusion.

- Read the story of the Ladder of Angels from Genesis 28:10-19.
- Show pupils the two images by Molly and Sam (pC2). These pictures give ideas about the meanings of the story.
- Discuss with pupils what might link heaven to earth. Consider the idea that the ladder comes down from heaven – but cannot be put up from earth.

This artistic approach can work for any story of faith. Artistic interpretations often open the window for pupils into the meaning of the text.

Learning with images

4 Glass, light and images

There are three images that show pupils' ideas about making stained glass designs. The moving expression of Hannah (pC3) is complemented by the extraordinary interfaith respect of Layla's work. Both show what 8-year-olds can do in thought and creativity. Jennie (pC12) takes the design and technology a stage further, and expresses the depths of her insight into the idea of God.

Show these three to pupils and introduce a way for them to create stained glass to express their own beliefs for themselves.

Jennie (14)

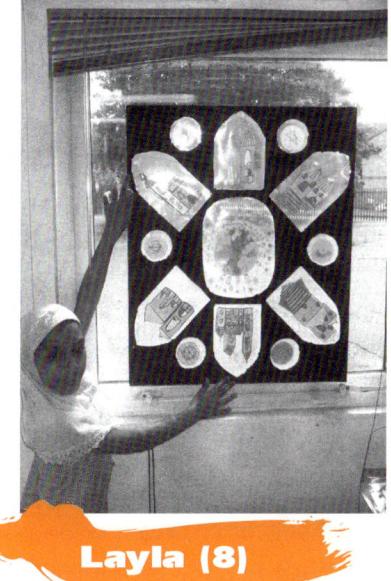
Layla (8)

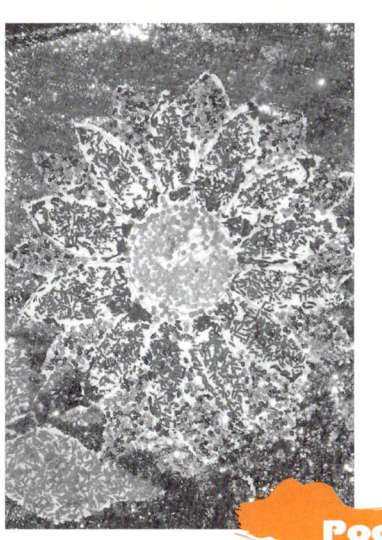
Pooja (11)

5 Patterns: expressing the spiritual

Pooja and Jennifer use lovely and detailed patterns to express their ideas. Patterning is a recognised kind of spiritual experience: when people say 'everything just fitted into place' or 'I was aware that I was in the flow...' then they are perhaps trying to describe the spiritual pattern of life.

Mosaics, sand patterns, repeating designs and calligraphy are often used to express an aspect of religious life. Look with pupils at the images of the Buddhist sand mandala, the Hindu rangoli and Islamic calligraphy.

Consider with pupils:
- Does their life have a pattern?
- Is it good to see the pattern of your life?
- How do these artistic patterns show something spiritual?

Rangoli pattern made from rice grains, seeds and pasta by students at Bournside School, Cheltenham © Martin Poyner

Inspiring Visual RE

6 Ideas about God

Paintings and artworks are a great way of engaging students to think more deeply about God.

A   Muslim expressions of the understanding of Allah

- Look with pupils at the images of Muslim belief about God.
- Discuss with pupils the Islamic rules that forbid making images of the divine. This is because any image of Allah would be false: for Muslims God is too great, too splendid, too far beyond our imagination for a picture to begin to do him justice. You might teach them the word 'transcendent'. This is why Islamic art uses patterns, beautiful writing, light, as a sign and text from the holy Qur'an to represent the divine.

B   God as love, balance, presence

Metaphors are an important part of our understanding and expression of ideas about God. Talk to pupils about some atheist metaphors:

- *If God was a garment it would be a hair shirt – irritating and pointless at the same time.*
- *If God was a food, it would be an emetic – it makes you sick.*
- *If God was a character in the movies it would be Santa – nice for the children, but pure fantasy.*

Look at the images made by Lloyd, Luke and Rowena. These three students have expressed their ideas about God through images of loving hearts, balancing good and evil, or finding God in your messy desk.

- What exactly do these young artists believe?
- How have they shown it?
- Are their ideas good?

C   For and against: comparing ideas about God

Paintings and artworks are a great way of engaging pupils taking GCSE or Standard Grade papers on the existence and nature of God.

- Compare Penny's vigorous rejection of the idea of God with Lloyd's vision of God as the love in all our hearts; Jennie's idea of God seen in the mirror of our own lives with Rowena's idea of finding God in the messy muddles of our lives. How do these images express beliefs and ideas?
- Ask pupils to think really hard about Inayah's idea that those who don't see God in the natural world are living with eyes closed. How would an atheist reply to this thinking?

Luke (13)

Inayah

11-14

Expressing beliefs in artistic ways: a focus on the question of evil

In this article, Liz Pope, head of RE, Advanced Skills Teacher and a Regional Subject Adviser for RE within the secondary curriculum developments, outlines an activity she developed with her Year nine pupils (aged 14–15).

Compelling learning experiences in RE contribute significantly to pupils developing a sense of meaning and purpose in life. They are usually prompted by a 'big question' and could take place in or out of school.

This activity uses artwork to encourage reflection and expression of pupils' own responses to a key question at the heart of human experience today and central to great learning in RE:

'Will the world ever be free of evil'?

Before the lesson.....

Gather the stimulus resources:

- **Stimulus A:** a copy of 'Satan, Sin and death' by William Blake. An internet image search reveals numerous website sources.
- **Stimulus B:** 'In the balance' artwork from Luke: NATRE's Spirited Arts Gallery 2007 (www.natre.org.uk).
- **Stimulus C:** 'God – he lies in you' artwork from Jenny: NATRE's Spirited Arts Gallery 2005.
- **Stimulus D:** Extracts from Milton's poem *Paradise Lost* (which inspired Blake), Book 2 Line 650ff and Line 666ff.

Do not introduce the topic or put the lesson aims and learning intentions or key questions onto the board. The students are going to produce these!

Provide each student with an A4 piece of plain paper. This will be their 'personal reactions board' where they express their thoughts and feelings – in words, colours, images, doodles. Kinaesthetic students can use modelling clay if more appropriate. This can be photographed if necessary.

Achievement

Students can demonstrate achievement at levels 5–7 in this work if they can say 'yes' to some of the following 'I can...' statements:

I can...

Level 5

- explain some responses to the problem of evil, using some religious and philosophical vocabulary
- express a personal response and show an awareness of others' views on the problem of evil.

Level 6

- give an informed account of some responses to the problem of evil, using religious and philosophical vocabulary
- express a reasoned personal response, showing some insight and consideration of others' views on the problem of evil.

Level 7

- show a coherent understanding of a range of responses to the problem of evil, using a wide range of religious and philosophical vocabulary in my explanations
- express personal responses and give critical evaluations of responses to the problem of evil.

**Stimulus A
'Satan, Sin and Death'
William Blake**

REtoday Services

Stimulus B   In the Balance

This is what Luke (13) said about his work:

'We believe that God is the balance of life. He is like the scales of justice, of good and bad. You can't have life without both sides because you wouldn't appreciate good without the bad. Some examples are night and day, illness and health, famine and harvest, suffering and joy, death and birth.

If God answered all prayers and no bad things occurred equilibrium would be lost and we would never learn from our mistakes. He is the ying and yang of our existence.'

Source: Spirited Arts website www.natre.org.uk. Navigate to 2007 gallery, 'Where is God?' section.

Stimulus C   God – He Lies In You

This is what Jennie (14) said about her work:

'People say that the presence of God is everywhere, I think that includes us. I believe that each and every one of us possesses Him. I have included a mirror as a centre piece: when one goes to look at this artwork, symbolizing God, they see their own face. The image will be broken, however, because it is hard to see that God is part of each one of us.

'Rays of yellow light, bringing a sense of happiness to the painting. Purple for the background as this symbolizes spirituality and inner power. I have painted blue round the mirror, a colour associated with heaven

'The design itself is like a stained glass window, something in a religious building like a church, often described as houses of God; I think this aspect of my design is quite significant.

'It is a very personal thing and I am sure that not everyone agrees with my opinion.

'This design has deep meanings; everything from the colour to the shapes used symbolizes something. I will not explain what I intend everything to mean, because I think this is what discovering the painting is about.

The main message my picture carries is that we can only use our own inner power, and inner spirits, to guide ourselves to a happier life to one day be accepted in whatever world awaits us after death.'

Source: Spirited Arts website www.natre.org.uk. Navigate to 2005 gallery, 'Where is God?' section.

Expressing beliefs in artistic ways

Stimulus D: Extracts from *Paradise Lost* by John Milton

The one seemed woman to the waist and fair,
But ended foul in many a scaly fold
Voluminous and vast, as serpent armed
With mortal sting: about her middle round
A cry of hell hounds never ceasing barked

Book 2 line 650ff

The other shape,
If shape it might be called that shape had none
Distinguishable in member, joint, or limb,
Or substance might be called that shadow seemed,
For each seemed either, black it stood as night,
Fierce as ten Furies, terrible as Hell,
And shook a dreadful dart; what seemed his head
The likeness of a kingly crown had on.

Book 2 line 666ff

1 Opening activity

Working in pairs or small groups, students need to *interpret, question* and *respond* to stimulus material.
Stimulus A, William Blake's painting 'Satan, Sin and Death'. Focus question: *Which is which? What makes you say this?* To assist, offer students extracts from Milton's *Paradise Lost* poem which inspired Blake (Stimulus D). More able students can use the original but other students would need a simplified version.
Stimulus B, Luke's artwork – give out without Luke's annotation. Focus question *What is he trying to express?*
Stimulus C, Jenny's artwork (without the annotation). Focus question: *What is she trying to express?*
Allow students time to express their responses on their 'personal reflection board'.
Encourage deeper reflection by asking

(a) Is there a theme or common idea in what they have expressed?
(b) Can they prioritise or choose the thought they would like to explore further?

Provide time for class discussion to

- share responses
- agree the key questions students want answers to.

2 Answering the key questions – analysing, researching and investigating

Working in groups, students are given one belief perspective on why there is evil in the world from the statements on p10.
They investigate, using ICT, local religious contacts or resources in school to develop their knowledge and understanding of that particular perspective, drawing on key religious teachings and key founders and leaders.
Findings need to be communicated on paper using a maximum number of 25 words. This could take the form of a mind map; a diagram; key words and pictures; or a poster.
Play 'Home and Away'. One student stays 'home', the rest of the group go 'away', one to each of the other groups. The 'home' student teaches the 'away' students about their viewpoint. Everyone then returns home and passes on what they have learnt. (Some teachers will know of this as the 'envoy' discussion strategy.)
If notes are necessary, the original work can be photocopied for students or put onto a Virtual Learning Environment (VLE) area.
Allow time for students to add to their 'personal reactions board' after the 'Home and Away' activity.

Why is there evil in the world?
Some perspectives from religion and belief

A Buddhist viewpoint

All life is suffering and caused by desire and selfishness. Follow the Buddha's path to reduce it.

An Agnostic (humanist) viewpoint

There is no proof that God does or doesn't exist. Humans need to fight evil and make the world a better place for everyone.

A Christian viewpoint

God gave everyone free will, and suffering is the consequence.

A Christian viewpoint

God allows evil and suffering for a reason – to help people develop into better people, to grow closer to God.

A Muslim viewpoint

Trust Allah. God is so great we can't know or understand the reasons for allowing evil and suffering. Life is a test and when things happen it is the will of Allah.

A Hindu viewpoint

Evil and suffering happen because of karma and reincarnation.

A Jewish viewpoint

People should struggle against evil by obeying God and keeping his commandments. If people did this then evil and suffering would decrease. People have to choose between good and evil.

3 Creative responses to the problem of evil – responding, expressing, evaluating and applying

The task – choose three different viewpoints to the problem of evil. Showing an understanding of the different viewpoints, critically respond, commenting on strengths and weaknesses, before making it clear what your personal response is.

Allow students to choose their preferred way of working from this list:

- **Art** – create a triptych (see below) Each panel is one viewpoint with their response. The middle panel is the one they feel most strongly about.
- **ICT** – create a 'YouTube' film (using Moviemaker, PowerPoint, etc). The images, words and music will express their response.
- **Poetry or drama dialogue** – picking up on the idea of Job's comforters in the book of Job in the Bible, have individual speakers giving their viewpoint on evil, with a Job character giving the personal response to each viewpoint.
- **Dance** – use movement to express how a person would respond if face to face with evil. What actions would they perform? How would they move? How would evil move? What actions would evil perform? How would you express your view – think about space, movement and contact work.

Some lend themselves better to individual work and others to group responses – allow the flexibility. These activities also offer opportunities to create links with other subject areas.

Year 9 Student feedback

'Can we do this again?'

'It was great being allowed to choose how we presented our work.'

'I liked being allowed to work with my friends.'

'I don't like not being allowed to write loads' (response following 'answering key questions' task).

'My head hurts.'

RE Today weblink

Additional materials, including full colour images and a dance/movement instruction sheet linked to this article are available for download by subscribers from the RE Today website. Go to www.retoday.org.uk. Enter the password found in your termly REtoday magazine) and click on curriculum resources.

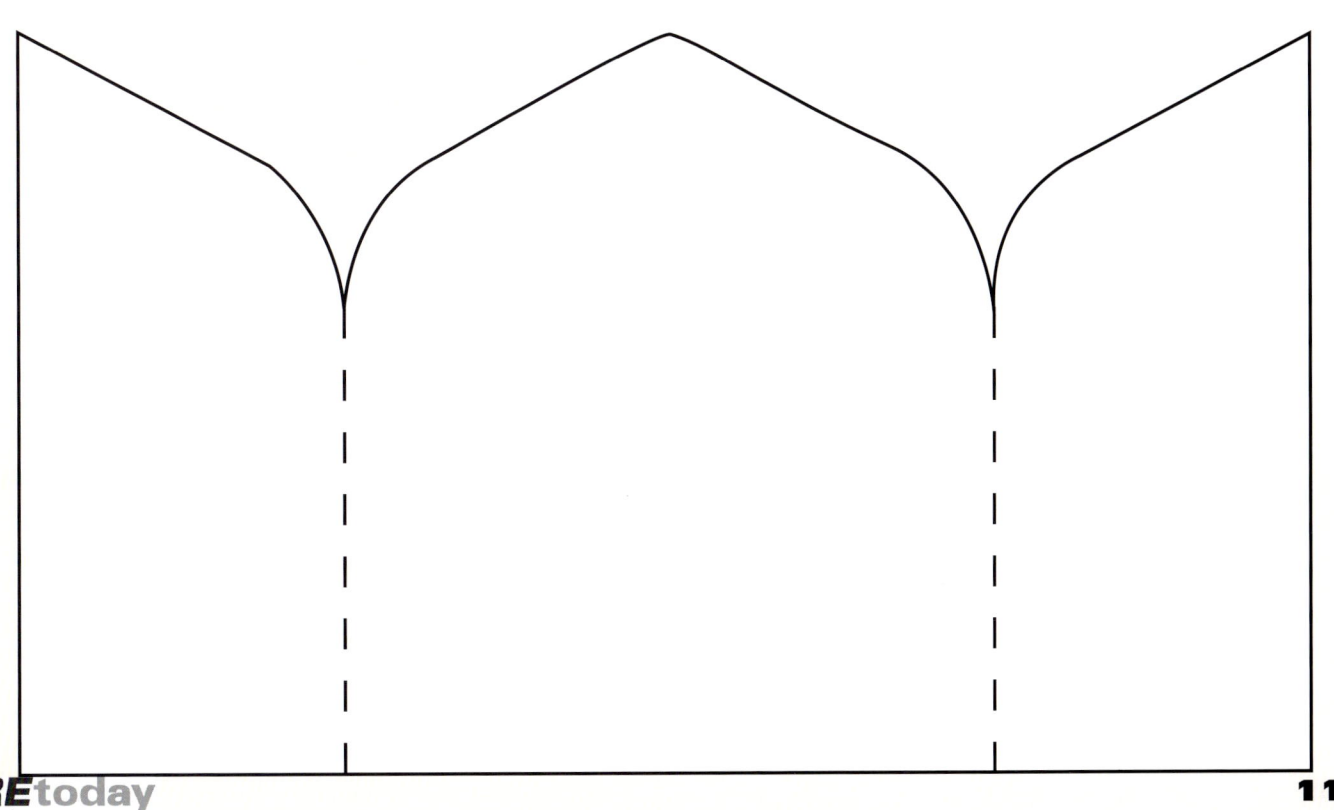

Creating art: eight simple ideas for the RE classroom

Good RE lessons often have a creative dimension to them: responding to the ways religions make things, pupils make something too. Here are eight ideas to energise your students' work, flexible across many religions for secondary age groups. The best work may have elements of design and art in it, but **the focus in RE will always be on the thinking and exploration of beliefs and their impact**. The eight ideas may suit 11–12 year olds: good teachers of RE adapt the learning to the pupil's age and needs.

Hands that talk

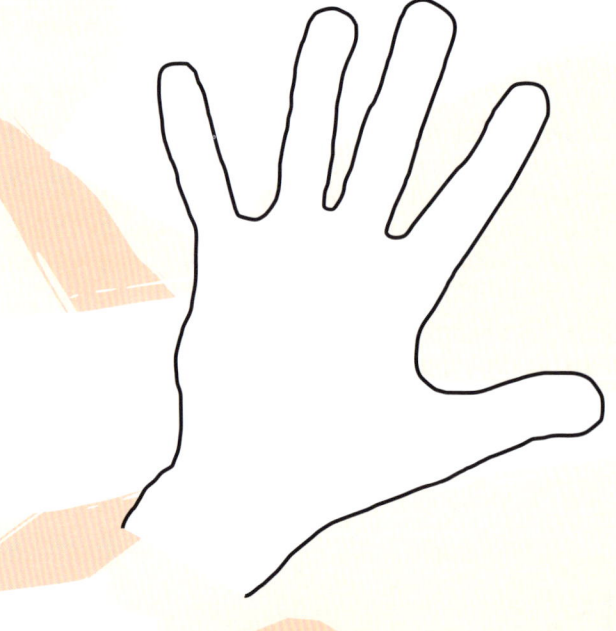

- Make the activity more meaningful by learning about different hand greetings – shake hands, high five, 'namaste', the North American indigenous 'How' greeting and many more. All are about sharing peace when we meet.
- Ask each pupil to make a two-sided hand, drawn round their own. On the fingers of one side they write five words naming things they do with their hands to be good, on the other side five things they regret doing with their hands
- Saint Paul wrote that 'true religion is not words or talk but action, love and power'. Ask pupils to write this, or another quotation of their choice, on the palm of both sides of their hand cut-out. Create a mobile of all the class's hands of action.

Create a story in the box

- Use some shoeboxes or copy-paper boxes for this activity. **Take a dramatic faith story**. Good examples might include Moses confronting Pharaoh, Jesus turning the tables over in the temple or the Four Sights of the Buddha.
- Using the box as if it were a TV screen, with one open side, pupils create in groups a range of tableaux **showing the key moments in the story**. One way of doing this is to use digital photographs as the back 'scenery' and create small card figures for the action. Set up the display of the different faith stories and tableaux for all to see around school.

Creating art: eight simple ideas

Crowd scene

All religions have stories in which crowds are significant. Pilgrimage to Makkah, the entry of Jesus into Jerusalem, the slaves escaping from Egypt, or the torrents of Hindu people flowing into the River Ganges at Varanasi are just a few examples.

- Ask each pupil to make a person who will become part of the crowd in a class work of art based on the story. This works well as a creative homework, inviting pupils to create the figure and bring it in. Some will give a lot of effort, and dress the character with fabric! Most pupils can create their own outline figure and design body language, costumes and facial expressions.
- Assemble the crowd scene on a large display board – some in the class gifted at art can add the other elements of an image. Then **give every student three speech or thought bubbles to go with the person they made**. Fill them in by answering these three questions:
    - What was I looking forward to about this event?
    - What was I thinking at the moment in the picture?
    - What will I remember from the day?
- Ask pupils to write an account of the feelings and experiences that go with the best crowd scene they have ever taken part in. Are football or pop concert crowds similar to or different from the religious or spiritual crowds studied?

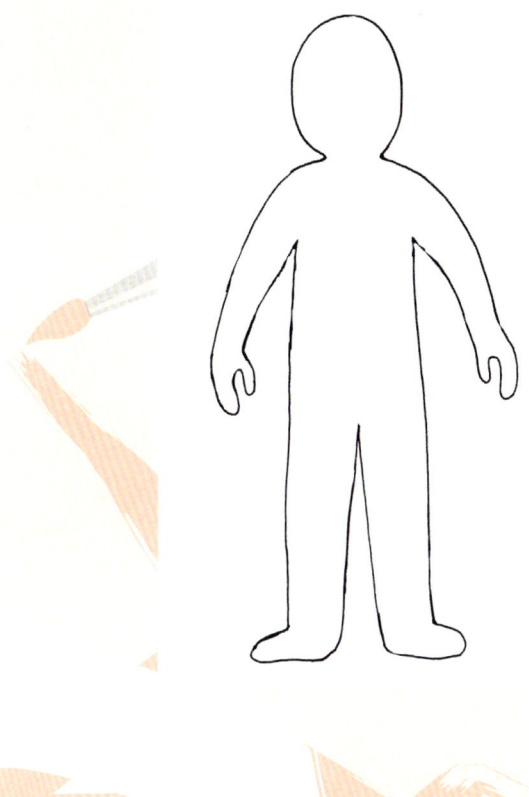

One beautiful word

Here is a Buddhist saying: 'Better than a thousand useless words is one word that brings peace.'

- Ask students to think of useless words, and give examples of these. Who do they know who uses lots of useless words (don't let them say it is teachers!)? Then ask them to think: what do they think is the one word that is most likely to bring peace?
- Give each student a piece of card – gold or silver is good, small is fine. Use the highest possible levels of calligraphic skill and the best resources to make the 'one beautiful word'. Collect all the words the pupils have made, and create a hanging display of '**words of peace**'. A mobile made from two coat hangers suspended from the classroom ceiling is a good way to display it.
- Ask pupils: are some words priceless? Is that the same as sacred? What might make a word holy? Do they have any holy words? What words from sacred writings appeal to them the most (you could give examples from which to choose)?

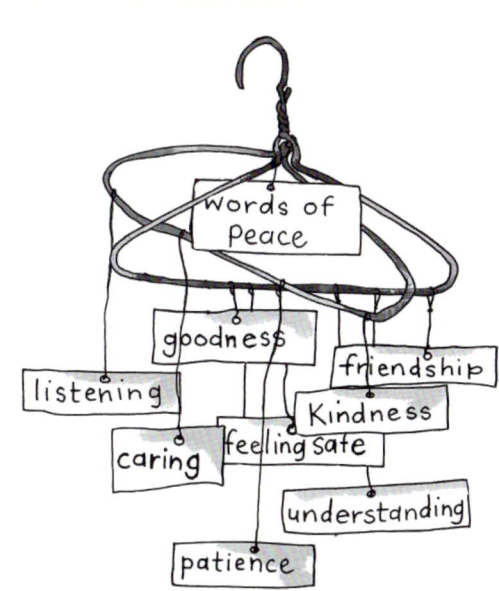

Camera, action

- **You will need:** enough digital cameras for groups of 4–6 to use one per group, or arrange to pass a smaller number around. A story from faith.
- Tell the story really well. Ask the groups to think about the **five key moments in the story**, and to **create tableaux images** of these key moments. Have one in the group to be photographer, one to be producer (s/he tells the others where to stand, how to pose, etc) and others to be key people in the story.
- When the photos have been taken, print them off and ask pupils to add speech and thought bubbles to complete the story, or this can be done digitally. Stories that work well with this strategy:
- Jacob wrestles the angel (Genesis 32:22-32)
- Siddhartha and the Swan (one source of this Buddhist story is http://www.sln.org.uk/storyboard/)
- Sita returns from exile in Lanka (from the Hindu Ramayana story)
- Jesus' disciples find the empty tomb (John ch 20 v.1-18).

PixSort: ranking images countdown

You will need: Christmas cards that show different aspects of the festival, from Santa and beer to frankincense, stables and the Madonna and Child.

- Give groups of pupils a selection of up to 10 of the Christmas cards to rank: which is closest to telling the true meaning of the festival?
- When groups have 10 pictures in rank order, and have had their say about 'why', invite any student to change two of the pictures, and give a reason. Keep going until the group more or less agree an order – but accept that this agreement is not final.
- Each group shares with the class their most and least meaningful cards and tells why.
- Ask **students to create an image of their own** which expresses what really matters at Christmas – for a Christian, or for themselves, or both. They might use three images, as it is hard to narrow down the meaning of Christmas to one thing.

Applying this to other religions: Flexible ways of working with this visual thinking activity might use 8 photos from Islam, 10 artefacts from Hinduism or 12 works of art related to stories of the Buddha. The ranking conversation, with the visual stimulus sets up the prioritising of the pupils' own responses.

Creating art: eight simple ideas

Taking a line for a walk on a tile

Islamic calligraphy uses geometric designs on tiles to explore the beautiful patterning of our lives and experiences. This activity will provide an opportunity to teach the class about the beauty of pattern, and the reasons why Muslims do not make images of humans – or of Allah.

- You will need: real tiles; alternatively thick car board squares will work well. On the left and right hand edges of each tile, mark the start of three lines of colour.
- Each pupil completes one or two tiles using the geometric shapes of Islamic art, then the class put all their tiles together in a mosaic. You will need some tiles to make the corners, marked with three lines on adjacent sides.

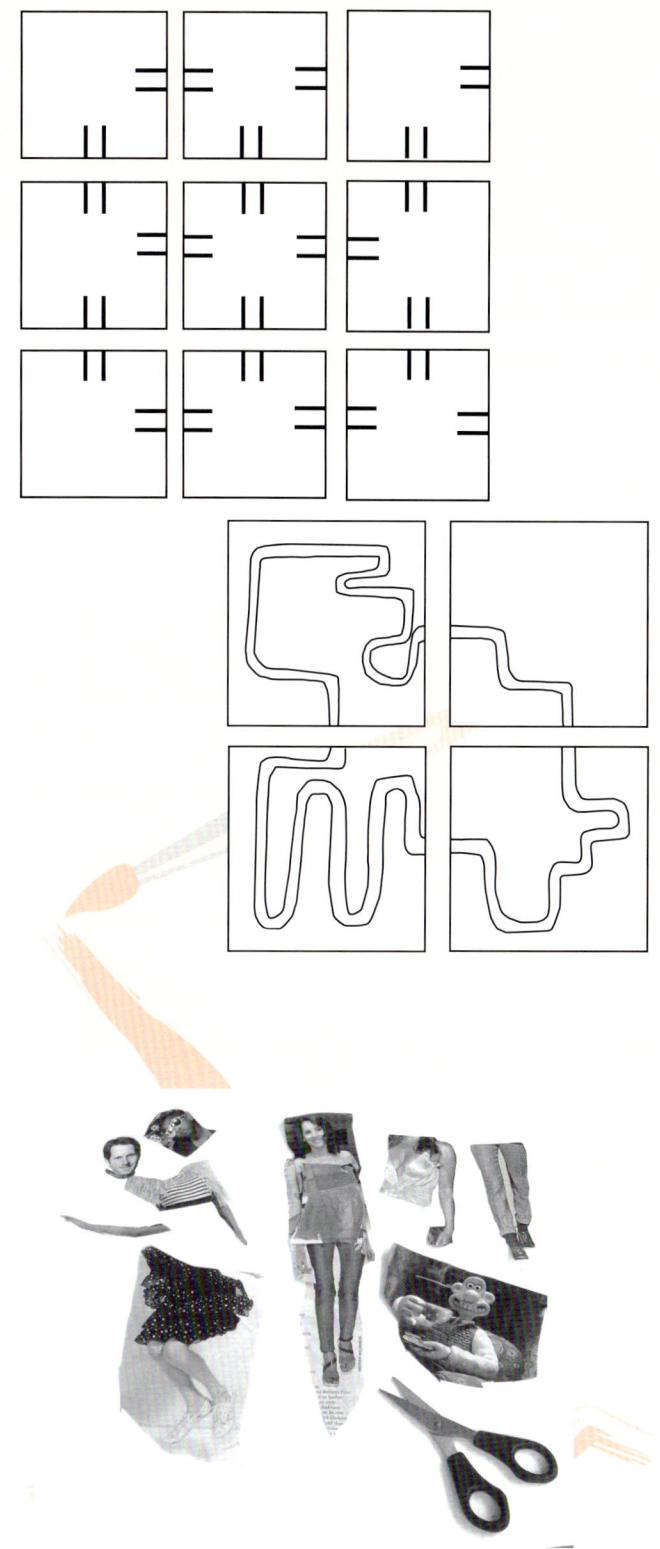

Whose head on whose body?

Introduce the activity by talking with pupils about the idea that religions teach that God created humanity. Talk together about what this means and consider the different ways God might have done this – through evolution, for example.

In this activity, pupils make composite images from magazine cuttings.

- Ask pupils in fours to use old magazines to cut out and collect lots of different body images. They will choose two eyes, a nose, a mouth, a hairstyle, a torso, two arms, two legs and so on. It works best if these are not too different in scale.
- Ask pupils to arrange these into odd juxtapositions. Ask them to create four images using the body parts they have collected – one weird, one peaceful, one excited and one other. Suggest they try out lots of different arrangements before anything is stuck down.
- Display these in a gallery round the class, and ask pupils: **If you made humanity, what nature would you give to the people? What differences would you include in them? What gifts of beauty or values would you give them?**

Why bother to make things in RE? Seven good reasons
Because....

- it is fun
- it makes learning more individual
- using different learning styles enables more pupils to achieve their best
- religions often craft, make and manufacture, so it can be an authentic window into faith community life
- making things is memorable
- there's usually too much reading and writing in RE lessons
- being creative and being spiritual are quite similar ways to be.

Art as meditation: sacred and secular

For the teacher

Art has been used to express ideas and insights for thousands of years. Art is often used in RE to enable pupils to develop their ability to interpret and understand religious beliefs. This unit, however, also pays attention to the value of *doing* art – the lessons that can be learnt from the *process* of producing art.

The processes outlined here focus on

1. getting students to produce their own **rangoli** patterns in order to help them to understand key beliefs in **Hinduism**, such as *karma* and *ahimsa*. Be inspired by a wonderful cross-curricular project at Bournside School in Cheltenham, where the production of a large **rangoli pattern** taught students and visitors about **Hindu** ideas of karma and reincarnation, as well as leading many into a time of deep reflection and contemplation.

2. the work of artist **Andy Goldsworthy**. This offers a way of using art as meditation, opening up a connection with the natural world. This approach suits him as a person with no institutional religious beliefs, but with a deep identification with nature. It would be pleasing to many religious believers too.

3. the use of **mandalas** to communicate beliefs. This meditative practice is an important part of **Mahayana Buddhism**. Students can devise their own mandalas in this activity.

The unit ends with an activity which draws on all three approaches and encourages students to produce their own expressive, meditative art.

In religion, mosaics, sand patterns, repeating designs and calligraphy are often used to express the spiritual.

The process is often as important as the outcome. This symmetrical pattern could be found in a Buddhist mandala or a Hindu rangoli.

Students can demonstrate achievement at levels 4–6 in this work if they can say 'yes' to some of the following 'I can...' statements:

I can...

Level 4

- suggest what a rangoli pattern or mandala means to a Hindu and a Buddhist
- **raise questions and suggest answers** to questions about impermanence and karma, suggested by rangoli, mandala and the work of Andy Goldsworthy.

Level 5

- **explain** how rangoli patterns and mandalas express a range of beliefs and point out the **similarities and differences** between them
- **ask questions and suggest answers** to questions of meaning raised by rangoli and mandalas, to do with our relationship with the natural world, consumerist values, impermanence, meditation.

Level 6

- **interpret** the significance of rangoli, mandala, and nature sculpture for different individuals and communities
- **express insights** into my own and others' beliefs about our relationship with the natural world, consumerist values, impermanence, meditation.

Art as meditation

RE, Art and Maths: rangoli and sacred geometry

Rangoli patterns are sometimes used in RE, particularly when associated with learning about the Hindu festival of Divali. However, rangoli patterns offer a rich resource as an engaging way in to a number of key Hindu beliefs. These pages offer a way of using rangoli as part of a wider project, linking RE, Art and Maths, as demonstrated by Bournside School, Cheltenham. Their theme was 'Full Circle' and their process is described below.

Planning the cross-curricular activity

1. **Link with your Art and Maths departments.** Identify areas of common interest and clarify aims and outcomes to satisfy the requirements of each partner subject. **The common interest found between the subjects** at Bournside was the way in which circles are powerful symbols, used to express ideas of infinity and eternity, as well as representing eyes, looking inwards and outwards, opening up gateways to the soul and to other worlds. They decided to focus on 'sacred geometry' in their linked project.

2. **Identify aims and outcomes that will satisfy the RE requirements.** At Bournside the key RE focus was on the concepts of 'expressing meaning' (AT1) and of 'exploring questions of meaning, purpose and truth' (AT2). Students learnt about Hindu beliefs underlying the geometrical designs of rangoli whilst engaged in the process of creating a rangoli. As they worked on the rangoli design, they explored questions of meaning and purpose, comparing Hindu spirituality with their own worldviews.

3. **Enable students to engage in the process.** Artist Ranbir Kaur worked with Religious Studies, Maths and Art students to produce a 12-foot square rangoli pattern on the floor of an art room. Students took responsibility for making the rangoli, creating a 'sacred space' around the installation using muslin drapes, producing suitable background music to encourage a meditative atmosphere, with some students filming the whole process.

4. **Explore the beliefs underpinning rangoli.** See p18. The full colour photograph is in the colour supplement, pC5. Subscribers can download a full-size version of the outline and the colour image from the RE Today website: www.retoday.org.uk.

5. **Recognise that the process of designing and producing the rangoli is a meditative act in its own right.** Both the process and the product encouraged a meditative, reflective response from both students involved and visitors to the exhibition. The careful placing of rice grains, seeds and pasta pieces required a slow, painstaking approach, slowing down the students and cultivating a total absorption with the process.

For information

- Rangoli is a traditional Hindu Indian use of art in the everyday.
- Rangoli patterns are created outside a home or temple daily, but are particularly associated with the festival of Diwali, where they are produced on the floor near the doorway to a home to welcome Lakshmi, the goddess of blessings and good fortune, and to encourage her to enter the home.
- Rangoli patterns are traditionally made with flour, rice or sand, seeds, pulses or lentils, often brightly dyed to make colourful designs.

Staff and visitors to the rangoli talked of the....

'wonder of patience in the process...'

'magnetic power of the art work...'

'going beyond the dimension of words...'

'sense of stillness.'

Exploring a Hindu rangoli pattern

In pairs...

1. Examine the line drawing of the rangoli pattern the students produced. Look at the key religious terms and identify where on the picture you think the rangoli expresses these beliefs. Explain how.
2. Write down at least five questions you would want to ask the artist about the rangoli and the beliefs behind it. How do you think he or she would answer?
3. How else might these ideas be expressed? Choose one or two of the beliefs and design an artwork to express it.
4. Talk together about the idea that life is transient and fleeting. List five things you might do and five things you would stop doing if you really took it seriously that life is short. What might you do differently if you believed in reincarnation?

Key terms

Reincarnation/transmigration: the individual soul (atman) passes through a series of lives in different species

Samsara: the cycle of life, death and rebirth of the soul until it attains moksha

Moksha: ultimate escape from the cycle of samsara, where the soul is released from the body and merges with God

Karma: the law of cause and effect – good or bad actions have good or bad consequences, affecting the soul's reincarnation

Transience: life is temporary, fleeting; it is part of an almost endless cycle, samsara

Ahimsa: respect for all life, compassion for all creatures

Art as meditation

Andy Goldsworthy: nature, art and meditation

Information file

The artist Andy Goldsworthy produces artwork using natural materials, usually in a natural setting. Often his work is **transient** – he creates structures that will be broken up by wind, waves and water, by decay and by new growth.

Goldsworthy's beautiful pieces reveal his deep identification with nature. While he professes no religious beliefs, he acknowledges that his work has a kind of **spiritual** purpose.

'Everything has the energy of its making inside it,' he says. 'There is no doubt that the internal space of a rock or a tree is important to me. But when I get beneath the surface of things, these are not moments of mystery, they are moments of extraordinary clarity.' (Interview with Tim Adams, *The Observer*, 11 March 2007)

Activities for students

1. Imagine that you work for an advertising agency. You have the job of persuading the following clients to use Goldsworthy to endorse a series of advertisements for them. What arguments might you give to support your view?

   Design an advert to demonstrate your points:

   (a) SAGE – Oxford's Christian Environmental Group

   (b) A Hindu Ahimsa Society

   (c) Freecycle – the worldwide network of groups who re-use and keep good stuff out of landfills.

2. 'Everything has the energy of its making inside of it ... But when I get beneath the surface of things, these are not moments of mystery, they are moments of extraordinary clarity.'

   - What do you think Goldsworthy means?
   - What do you think he sees or understands at these moments?
   - Choose an image of his art and reflect on how he has made it, the process he undertook and how he might feel before, during and after.
   - Then write what you think his 'moment of extraordinary clarity' might be.

3. Which of the following quotations do you think Goldsworthy will most identify with and why? Which view(s) might he reject and why?

   (a) 'The earth is the Lord's and everything in it.' (Psalm 24 verse 1)

   (b) 'Know that all opulent, beautiful and glorious creations spring but from a spark of (Krishna's) splendour.' (*Bhagavad Gita*, Chapter 10)

   (c) 'Humankind has not woven the web of life. We are but one thread within it. Whatever we do to the web, we do to ourselves. All things are bound together. All things connect.' (Chief Seattle)

   (d) 'Spend, spend, spend!' (Vivian Nicholson)

4. Why do people cling to stuff? Does Goldsworthy have a message for religious people as well as non-religious?

Using a mandala for quiet reflection

Information file

In Mahayana Buddhism, a **mandala or sacred circle** serves to portray the home of a specific holy being. They can be temporary, made of sand, rice or coloured powders. These mandalas are swept away as a reminder of **impermanence**. Sand mandalas may be gathered up and placed in running water in order to spread the blessing accrued. Some mandalas are more permanent, painted on a hanging scroll.

The mandala is traditionally a plan view of a temple, with four gateways. The meditator can visualise her- or himself entering the mandala, coming to a palace at the centre, which can represent the temple of her or his own heart.

See also A Buddhist mandala was created at the Bath Museum of Eastern Asian Art in October 2008. For an online photo story go to http://www.meaa.org.uk/monksdaily.html

© Museum East Asian Art 2008. Used by permission.

Activity: Draw your own mandala

This activity is intended to give students a sense of how constructing a mandala can be a meditative process. It will be important to agree appropriate ground rules for any reflective activity as an essential starting point, such as making it clear that their responses can remain private if they wish.

1. Set quiet atmosphere with background music.
2. Give out template and pens.
3. Ask pupils to focus on the centre of their page and on a word, such as 'hope' or 'purpose'.
4. Tell students to draw whatever comes to mind, repeating it as a pattern around the centre of the page. Put their thoughts into lines, colours or symbols.
5. Point out that it is easier to repeat the patterns if they rotate the paper.
6. They can take their time; there are no rules – if they run out of ideas they can stop and reflect.
7. They can consider the idea of placing things they'd like to leave behind 'outside the walls of my heart' – at the edges of the paper.

This exercise can help pupils to become aware of how they are thinking and feeling. This can be the starting point for developing understanding of the value of meditation.

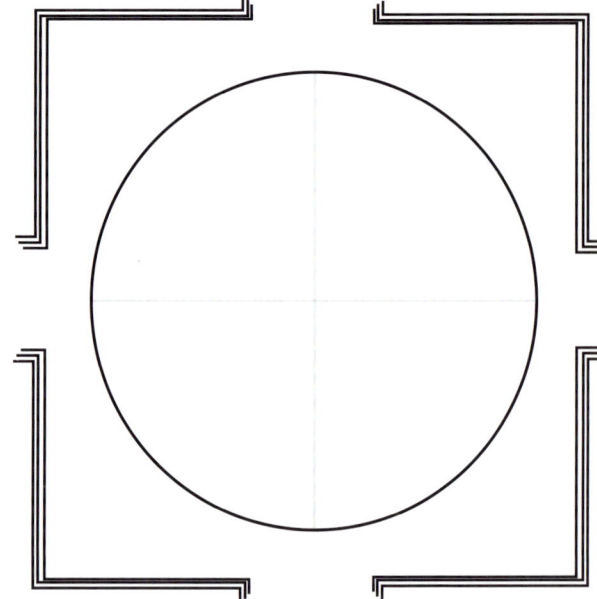

Individual reflection
How did you feel? What title would you give your mandala? Why? Did it reveal what is going on inside your heart? Is that important?

Pairs
Describe your mandala to a partner. Invite comment from your partner if you wish. You may prefer to keep it private.

Whole class discussion
What are the benefits of slowing down and thinking like this? Is it important to keep in touch with your inner self? What happens when you do and when you don't? What difference will this make to you? What will you do as a result of this reflection?

Art as meditation

Drawing out the learning

For the teacher

The previous pages introduce three approaches to using art in a meditative way to express beliefs, values and ideas. The following activities suggest ways of drawing out some higher-level learning from students. The focus here is on enabling pupils to consider the similarities and differences between these three approaches. Use the similarities and differences framework on p22 to help students to think about the issues and frame their responses. Select from the following tasks to allow students to produce responses that meet the 'I can' statements on p13.

Activities for students

1. Imagine a conversation between
   - Shivani – a Hindu student from the Bournside *rangoli* project
   - Andy Goldsworthy
   - one of the monks from the Museum of East Asian Art mandala workshop.

   In groups of three, using the similarities and differences sheet, write down or act out the conversation, explaining ways in which the art expresses different beliefs.

2. Imagine that your local Council is holding a competition to choose one art form that is most relevant for a 'Life in the Twenty-First Century' display at the local town hall.
   - In groups, do more research into the three art forms and the beliefs they express.
   - Choose two students to represent each art form. These representatives have to make a presentation to the Council to explain why their art form – rangoli, nature sculpture or mandala – should be chosen as expressing what is important about being human in 21st-century Britain. They should consider what messages the art puts across about religious beliefs, our relationship with our environment, sustainability, human nature, values, happiness and meaning.
   - The class can then vote as to which artwork should be chosen. Each student must give reasons for his or her choice.

3. Choose the art form that most speaks to you. Write a letter to Shivani, Andy Goldsworthy or a Buddhist monk to explain what has impressed you most about their artwork. Use at least six of the following sentence starters in your letter:
   - What struck me most about your work was...
   - The thing that appeals to me...
   - I was surprised to see that...
   - I agree with you about...
   - I have a different viewpoint about...
   - My interpretation of what you are trying to say in your work is...
   - I understand that your work expresses belief in...
   - I imagine that this is important to you because...
   - I think that it is more important to believe that...
   - Learning about your art has made me...
   - One thing that I will do from now on is...

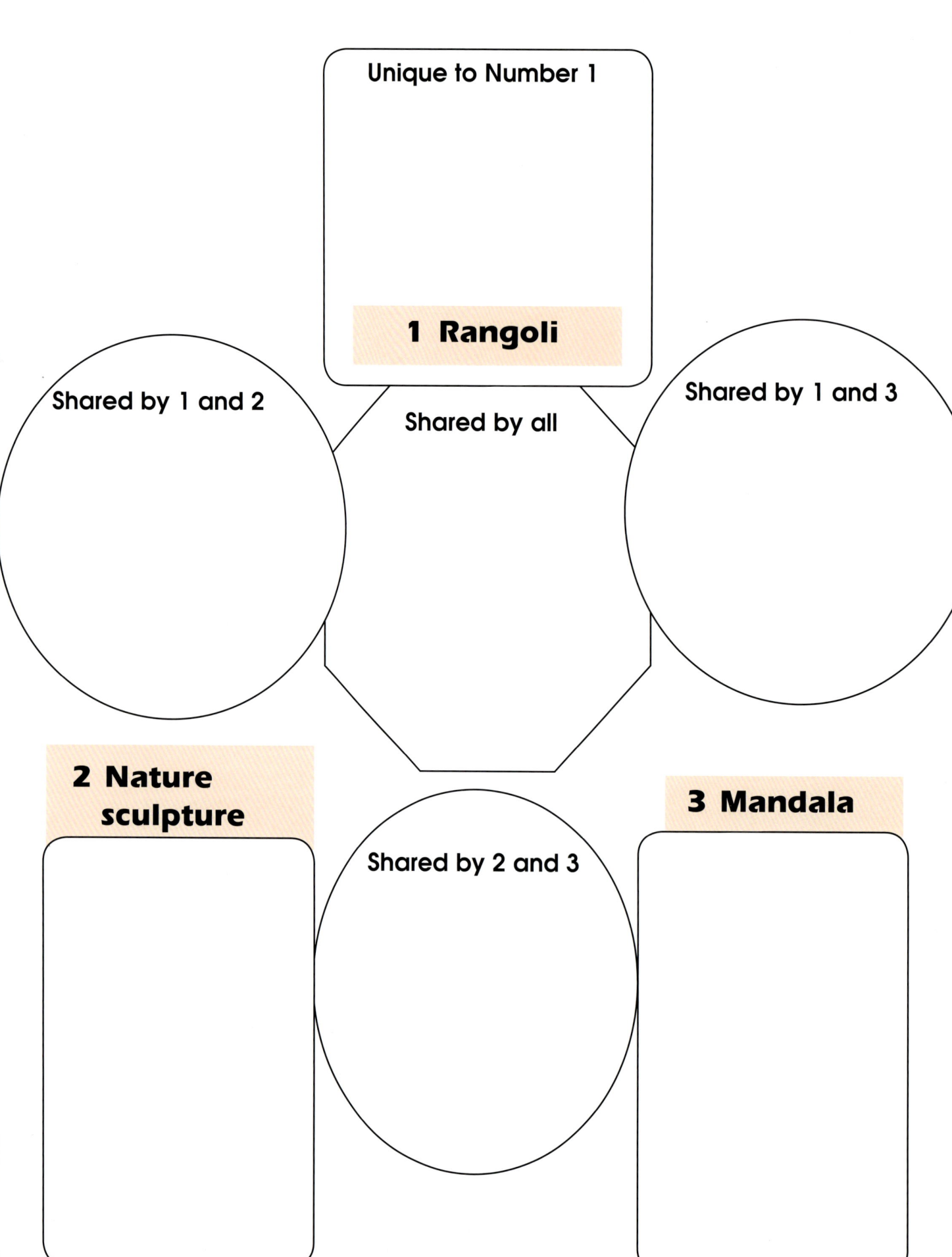

Recognising achievement and attainment in creative and artistic RE

Approaches to RE that emphasise the creative, reflective and imaginative aspects of the subject are attractive to teachers and students alike, but teachers are anxious: is there time for these kinds of RE when attainment targets must be met? The tension is real, but can be resolved.

With careful task setting, good achievement in RE can be demonstrated just as surely through use of creative expression as through a piece of writing or examples of philosophical analysis. Good task setting begins with clarity about the outcomes being aimed for.

The table below demonstrates how some of the QCA eight-level scale statements can be expressed in pupil-friendly 'I can…' statements based upon some of the activities in this book.

Develop and use 'I cans' such as these for your RE and both you and your students will be able to say how well they are doing!

Level	Pupils show their learning from religion by…	In RE in practice, evidence might come from…
3	• **making links** between what religious communities create and their own lives, questions and ideas.	• **asking three good questions** about a religious work of art and three good questions about a work of art they think is spiritual.
4	• showing that they **understand** some creative ways beliefs are expressed • **applying some ideas** about art, imagination or creativity to religious questions.	• **expressing understanding** of three different forms of religious expression (e.g. hymns, architecture, art) • **creating** a thoughtful work of art of their own that **applies** an idea such as 'spiritual' or 'vision' or 'open minded'.
5	• **explaining the impact** of creative expression of meaning in religious and community life • **expressing views** thoughtfully about a diverse range of spiritual expressions.	• **giving good reasons why** the expression of faith in hymns, art, architecture and stained glass matter to Christians • **expressing their view** of a question about God in an artistic way, with attention to questions of meaning, purpose and truth.
6	• **interpreting** spiritual/religious ways of expressing meaning in different forms, with reference to religious sources • **expressing** their own insights into creative responses to questions of meaning, purpose and truth.	• **using ideas** like 'the numinous' or 'divine guidance' or 'inspiration' **to interpret** religious phenomena • **creating an insightful work** of art and commentary on it to express their own sense of vision or inspirations.
7	• **giving critical and personal evaluations** of diverse expressions of religious and spiritual ideas • **using a wide creative vocabulary effectively to account** for their own religious and/or spiritual expressions of meaning.	• **evaluating diverse expressions of religious meaning** found in the work of William Blake and Damian Hirst both critically and personally • creating a coherent, insightful work of art and commentary to **express their own sources and ideas** of vision and inspiration.

Many of the artworks from students featured in this resource show evidence of achievement in line with the statements in the table. Many students will be able to show good levels of RE achievement in their creative work. These usually refer to AT2, learning from religion, but the best RE will also incorporate students' developing understanding of particular religious ideas as well, entwining AT1 and 2 together.

SPIRITED ARTS

The National Association of Teachers of RE has run an annual competition for more creative RE since 2004. Many thousands of young people of all ages and abilities have entered their work in the Art in Heaven competition and the web gallery showcases some of the best. See: www.natre.org.uk/spiritedarts

The following outlines are just some of those provided for the competition over the years. Use them to start your pupils thinking. What might they produce? What ideas and insights linked to their learning in RE could they express? A picture or 3D creative piece linked to a theme, together with a clear explanation, is the aim.

Telling it My Way: Stories of Faith

In this theme, any faith story being studied in RE can be explored or analysed by pupils who express their own ideas and insights into the story. They might ask 'Where does a turning point occur in the story?' or 'What makes this story popular?' or 'What impact does this story have today?'

Some will respond to Moses, the Prophet Muhammad ﷺ, the Gurus, the stories of Jesus or the Buddha.

Others will make spiritual links to the Prodigal Son, *The Lion, the Witch and the Wardrobe* or the life of Gandhi. A profound image, with a clear explanation, will go far!

Where is God?

Invite pupils to think about the question 'Where is God?'

Some stories from the faith communities answer this question. Many pupils will have their own answers. Agnostics and atheists may say 'we don't know' or 'nowhere'.

Winning work in this area mixes elements such as talking about God – or to God – doubt, theology, seeking, sensing or listening to God creatively. Pupils' own views, and the answers of one or more religions, both have a place.

My Spiritual Life

In this theme, pupils might think of the meaning of spiritual life for them. Is it about prayer, or doing justice? Worship, or helping others? What is the spiritual life of their local faith communities? Or of the non-religious? And how do they see their own spirit, their own spirituality? A spiritual image, and a written reflection on what makes it spiritual, will be a winning combination.

All of the images referred to in this publication can be found in the colour supplement and also on the RE Today website (for subscribers).